This Journal Belongs To:

Drow your family tree

Made in the USA
Coppell, TX
22 January 2020

14869229R00072